Better Homes and Gardens®

CHEESE RECIPES

Our seal assures you that every recipe in *Cheese Recipes*
has been tested in the Better Homes and Gardens® Test Kitchen.
This means that each recipe is practical and reliable,
and meets our high standards of taste appeal.

For years, Better Homes and Gardens® Books has been a leader in publishing cook books. In *Cheese Recipes,* we've pulled together a delicious collection of recipes from several of our latest best-sellers. These no-fail recipes will make your cooking easier and more enjoyable.

Editor: Rosemary C. Hutchinson
Editorial Project Manager: Rosanne Weber Mattson
Graphic Designer: Harijs Priekulis
Electronic Text Processor: Paula Forest

On the front cover: Chutney Cheese Ball *(see recipe, page 6)*

Contents

Taco-Beef Dip

1 pound lean ground beef 1 clove garlic, minced	● In a 10-inch skillet cook ground beef and garlic till beef is browned. Drain fat.	By using your microwave oven, you'll have this spicy dip ready in next to no time. In a nonmetal casserole dish micro-cook the ground beef and garlic on 100% power (HIGH) for 4 to 5 minutes, stirring once to break up the meat. Drain off fat. Stir in tomato sauce, taco seasoning mix, and pepper sauce. Cook for 3 minutes. Toss cheese with flour. Gradually stir into meat mixture. Cook for 2 to 3 minutes, stirring every 30 seconds, or till heated through and cheese melts. Serve as directed at left.
1 15-ounce can tomato sauce ½ of a 1¼-ounce envelope taco seasoning mix (about 2 tablespoons) Several dashes bottled hot pepper sauce	● Stir in tomato sauce, taco seasoning mix, and hot pepper sauce. Simmer, uncovered, for 5 minutes.	
2 cups shredded cheddar *or* Monterey Jack cheese (8 ounces) 1 tablespoon all-purpose flour	● Toss cheese with flour. Add cheese to meat mixture, a little at a time, stirring just till melted.	
Dairy sour cream 1 small tomato, chopped 1 tablespoon sliced green onion Tortilla *or* corn chips	● Transfer the hot mixture to a fondue pot or chafing dish, then place over the burner. Dollop with sour cream. Garnish with tomato and green onion. Serve with tortilla or corn chips. Makes 3½ cups.	

Attention, Microwave Owners

Microwave recipes were tested in countertop microwave ovens that operate on 600 to 700 watts. Cooking times are approximate since microwave ovens vary by manufacturer. If yours has fewer watts, foods may take a little longer to cook.

Keeping hot dips hot
needn't be a problem.
Here are some
suggestions to help you
avoid running back and
forth to the kitchen.

Heat and keep food
warm in a fondue pot or
an electric slow crockery
cooker. Or, heat the dips
on the stove and transfer
them to a ceramic pot or a
clay pot—both hold heat a
long time. Still another
option is to place the
serving container on an
electric hot tray to keep
the dip warm.

P.S. Reheating dips
goes faster if you remove
them from the refrigerator
about 30 minutes before
serving.

Salmon Supreme Ball

1	8-ounce package cream cheese
1	cup shredded cheddar cheese (4 ounces)
1	7¾-ounce can salmon, drained, boned, and finely flaked
½	teaspoon dried dillweed
¼	cup onion salad dressing

● Bring cream cheese and cheddar cheese to room temperature. In a mixer bowl beat cheeses, salmon, and dillweed with an electric mixer till combined. Gradually add the onion salad dressing, beating till fluffy. Cover and chill for several hours or overnight. (May be stored up to 5 days.)

Save money by buying pink or chum salmon rather than the more expensive red varieties.

Snipped parsley
Assorted crackers

● Before serving, shape salmon mixture into a ball or log, then roll in parsley. Serve with crackers. Makes 1 ball or log (about 2½ cups).

Chutney Cheese Ball

2	cups shredded sharp cheddar cheese (8 ounces)
2	tablespoons butter *or* margarine
⅓	cup milk
1	teaspoon Worcestershire sauce
	Dash bottled hot pepper sauce
⅓	cup finely chopped chutney

● Bring cheese and butter or margarine to room temperature. In a mixer bowl beat with an electric mixer till combined. Add milk, Worcestershire sauce, and hot pepper sauce, beating till combined. Stir in chutney. Cover and chill for several hours or overnight.

Pictured on the cover.

Ball, log, circle, heart—shape this peppy cheese mixture to fit your mood or the occasion.

⅓ cup finely chopped pecans
   or peanuts
Assorted crackers *or*
   vegetable dippers

● Before serving, shape cheese mixture into a ball, then roll in pecans or peanuts. Serve with crackers or vegetable dippers. Makes 1 ball (about 2 cups).

Baked Brie with Strawberries

1   1- to 1½-pound unsliced round loaf whole grain bread
1   1½- to 2-pound round Brie cheese with rind, 6 to 8 inches in diameter
    Fresh strawberries
    Apple slices
    Lemon juice

● Slice ½ inch off the top of the bread and save for another use. Cut loaf as directed at right. If necessary, trim cheese into a circle 2 inches smaller than the diameter of the bread. Insert cheese into bread, then wrap in foil. Bake in a 350° oven about 30 minutes or till heated through. Top with strawberries and apple slices dipped in lemon juice. Slice into wedges to serve. Serves 16 to 20.

To make a bread shell, insert toothpicks in a circle around the top of the cut loaf, 1 inch from the edge. Use a serrated knife to cut down through the loaf around the toothpicks, leaving a base 1 inch thick. Use your fingers to gently remove the center.

Use your microwave oven to make baked Brie without the bread.
Place one 4½-ounce round Brie cheese, rind removed, in a small nonmetal shallow baking dish. Sprinkle with broken *pecans or walnuts.* Micro-cook, uncovered, on 100% power (HIGH) about 30 seconds or till the cheese begins to melt and lose its shape. Serve immediately with fresh fruit or unsalted crackers.

Fried Cheese and Broccoli

1 8-ounce package cream cheese 2 cups shredded sharp cheddar cheese (8 ounces)	● Bring cream cheese and cheddar cheese to room temperature. In a medium mixer bowl beat cheeses with an electric mixer till combined.
1½ cups broccoli *or* cauliflower flowerets	● Mold about *1 tablespoon* cheese mixture around *each* floweret. Cover and chill wrapped flowerets about 1 hour.
1 slightly beaten egg 1 cup all-purpose flour 1 cup milk 2 tablespoons cooking oil	● For batter, in a medium bowl combine egg, flour, milk, and cooking oil. Beat with a rotary beater just till combined. Carefully dip each chilled broccoli or cauliflower floweret into batter.
Cooking oil for deep-fat frying	● In a heavy saucepan fry flowerets, a few at a time, in deep hot oil (365°) for 2 to 3 minutes or till golden brown. Drain on paper towels. Serve warm. Makes about 36 pieces.

Enhance your reputation as a great cook by serving this unique appetizer—fresh vegetables wrapped in cheese, dipped in batter, and deep-fried. Be sure you have plenty!

Fry a few pieces at a time in hot oil. The size of your deep-fat fryer or heavy saucepan will determine the number of pieces you can fry at a time. Drain the cooked vegetables before serving.

Pat flowerets dry with paper towels so cheese mixture will stick. You may need a little more or a little less than 1 tablespoon of cheese, depending on the size of your vegetable pieces.

Just before you're ready to fry the vegetable pieces, dip them into the batter. Let excess batter drip off before you put them into the hot oil.

Crowded Canoes

1 celery stalk Any flavor cheese spread	● Rinse celery and pat dry with a paper towel. Cut into three equal pieces. Mound cheese spread into celery pieces.
1 to 2 tablespoons crisp rice cereal *or* corn puff cereal	● Spread the cereal on waxed paper. Gently press the celery pieces, cheese side down, into the cereal. Makes 3.

This simple snack is ideal for kids to make themselves. Our child testers just loved it. They told us to tell you peanut butter works great, too.

Pirate's Treasure

¾ cup all-purpose flour 1 5-ounce jar American cheese spread ¼ cup butter *or* margarine, softened	● In a medium mixing bowl combine flour, cheese spread, and softened butter or margarine. Mix with your hands till well combined.
1 cup corn flakes, finely crushed (½ cup)	● Spread crushed corn flakes on a piece of waxed paper. Shape cheese mixture into 1-inch balls by rolling small amounts between palms of hands. Roll in crushed corn flakes to coat. Place about 2 inches apart on an ungreased cookie sheet. With the bottom of a drinking glass, flatten balls to ¼-inch thickness. Bake in a 375° oven about 12 minutes or till edges are lightly browned. Makes 24.

These crisp cheese wafers are a tasty snack for hard-to-please little ones. Small hands can help mix the dough because it's soft but not sticky.

Three Blind Mice Crackers

4 slices melba toast 6 whole pitted olives, halved lengthwise; 3 cherry tomatoes, quartered; *or* 12 whole almonds	● Place melba toast slices on a baking sheet. For mice, arrange *three* olive halves, tomato quarters, or whole almonds on *each* slice of melba toast.	**MICROWAVE TIMING** Place cheese-topped crackers on a nonmetal plate. Micro-cook on HIGH (100%) power for 30 seconds or till cheese is melted. Remove and insert chow mein noodles for tails.
2 slices American cheese Chow mein noodles	● Cut cheese slices in half to fit melba toast. Place a cheese strip atop "mice" on melba toast. Broil about 4 inches from heat for 1 to 3 minutes or till cheese melts. Insert a chow mein noodle under cheese near each "mouse" for tails. Makes 4.	

Tiny Cheddar Cheese Balls

1 3-ounce package cream cheese, softened ½ cup shredded cheddar *or* mozzarella cheese ¼ cup sunflower nuts	● In a small mixing bowl combine cream cheese and shredded cheddar or mozzarella cheese till well mixed. Stir in sunflower nuts. Shape cheese mixture into 1-inch balls.	**Keep these tempting tidbits in the refrigerator for the next time you get hungry between meals.**
¼ to ⅓ cup Grape Nuts cereal	● Place the Grape Nuts cereal in a bowl. Roll each cheese ball in cereal till it is coated. Serve at once or store in a tightly covered container in the refrigerator for up to 3 days. Makes 12.	

Layered Cheese and Pesto

Pesto Filling	● Prepare Pesto Filling. Set aside.	Pesto usually is tossed with hot cooked pasta or vegetables. But we've put it between layers of rich cheeses and cream for this dramatic spread.
1 **8-ounce package cream cheese** 1 **4½-ounce round Camembert *or* Brie cheese, rind removed** ½ **cup whipping cream**	● Bring cream cheese and Camembert or Brie cheese to room temperature. In a small mixer bowl beat cheeses together with an electric mixer till nearly smooth. In a small mixing bowl beat whipping cream till soft peaks form. Fold whipped cream into cheese mixture.	
	● Line a 3½- to 4-cup mold with plastic wrap. Spread *one-fourth* of the cheese mixture into prepared mold. Spread *one-third* of the Pesto Filling over the cheese mixture. Repeat cheese and pesto layers twice more. Spread remaining cheese mixture on top. Cover and chill for several hours or overnight.	
Paprika (optional) **Fresh basil** **Assorted crackers *or* French bread**	● Before serving, invert mold onto a serving plate. Remove mold and carefully peel off plastic wrap. Sprinkle with paprika, if desired. Garnish with basil. Serve with crackers or thin slices of French bread. Makes 3½ cups.	
	● **Pesto Filling:** In a blender container or food processor bowl combine 1 cup firmly packed snipped *fresh basil;* ¾ cup grated *Parmesan or Romano cheese;* ½ cup firmly packed snipped *parsley;* ¼ cup *pine nuts, walnuts, or almonds;* and 2 cloves *garlic,* quartered. Cover and process with several on/off turns till a paste forms. (Stop machine occasionally to scrape down sides.) With machine running slowly, gradually add ⅓ cup *olive oil or cooking oil* and process to the consistency of soft butter. Makes about 1 cup.	If fresh basil is hard to come by, use all snipped *parsley* for this pesto (a total of 1½ cups firmly packed). Then add 1 teaspoon dried *basil,* crushed, and continue as directed.

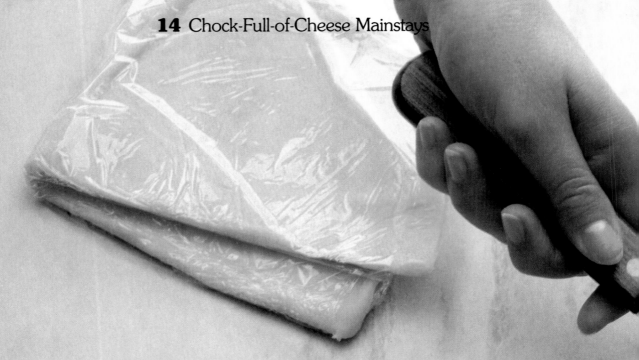

Bacon-Cheddar Quiche

½ **15-ounce package folded refrigerated unbaked piecrusts (1 crust)**
6 **slices bacon**

● Let piecrust stand at room temperature for 15 to 20 minutes according to package directions. Meanwhile, cook bacon till crisp; drain on paper towels. Crumble bacon.

This no-measure quiche can be shortcut even more. Simply substitute ¼ cup bacon bits for the cooked bacon and 1 tablespoon dried minced onion for the green onions.

3 **beaten eggs**
1 **12-ounce can (1½ cups) evaporated milk**
1 **4-ounce package shredded cheddar cheese**
3 **green onions, thinly sliced**

● In a mixing bowl combine eggs and milk. Stir in cheese, onions, and bacon.
　Place piecrust in a 9-inch pie plate. Flute edges high. Line crust with a layer of heavy-duty foil. Bake in a 450° oven for 5 minutes. Carefully remove foil from piecrust and bake about 5 minutes more or till piecrust is nearly done. Remove piecrust from the oven. Reduce the oven temperature to 325°.

● Pour egg mixture into *hot* piecrust. Bake in a 325° oven for 30 to 35 minutes or till a knife inserted near the center comes out clean. Let stand 10 minutes before serving. Makes 6 servings.

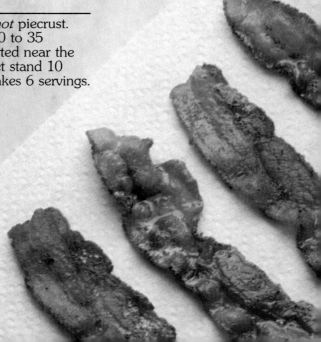

Chorizo-Tortilla Casserole

½ **pound bulk chorizo** *or* **Italian sausage** 1 **medium onion, chopped** 5 **6-inch corn tortillas**	● In a medium saucepan cook meat and onion till meat is brown and onion is tender. Drain off fat. Meanwhile, cut tortillas into strips about 3 inches long and ½ inch wide.
1 **10-ounce can tomatoes and green chili peppers** 1 **6-ounce can tomato juice** ½ **teaspoon sugar** ½ **teaspoon dried oregano, crushed** ¼ **teaspoon pepper**	● Stir tomatoes and chili peppers, juice, sugar, oregano, and pepper into meat mixture. Bring to boiling; reduce heat. Cover. Simmer for 5 minutes; remove from heat. Stir in tortilla strips.
¼ **cup shredded cheddar** *or* **Monterey Jack cheese (1 ounce)** **Fresh cilantro** *or* **parsley sprigs (optional)**	● Spoon meat mixture into a 1-quart casserole. Cover and refrigerate up to 24 hours. 　Cover and bake in a 350° oven about 50 minutes or till heated through. Sprinkle with cheese. Bake, uncovered, for 2 to 3 minutes more or till cheese melts. Garnish with fresh cilantro or parsley, if desired. Makes 4 servings.

Chorizo (chuh REE zoh) is a highly spiced sausage that's popular in Mexican cooking. Look for it at ethnic markets.

Microwave Method: In a 1-quart nonmetal casserole micro-cook meat and onion, uncovered, on 100% power (high) for 3 to 5 minutes or till meat is brown and onion is tender, stirring once to break up meat. Drain off fat. Meanwhile, cut tortillas into strips 3 inches long and ½ inch wide.

　Stir tomatoes and green chili peppers, tomato juice, sugar, oregano, and pepper into meat mixture. Cook, covered, on high about 5 minutes or till bubbly, stirring once. Stir in tortillas. Cover and refrigerate several hours or overnight.

　Cook, covered, on 70% power (medium-high) for 10 to 15 minutes or till heated through, stirring once. Sprinkle with cheese. Cook on high about 1 minute or till cheese melts. Garnish with fresh cilantro or parsley, if desired.

Caper Burgers

1 beaten egg 2 tablespoons plain yogurt ¼ cup fine dry bread crumbs Dash pepper 1 pound lean ground beef *or* pork	● In a medium mixing bowl combine egg and yogurt. Stir in bread crumbs and pepper. Add ground meat and mix well. Shape the meat mixture into eight ¼-inch-thick patties.
3 tablespoons capers 1 tablespoon brown mustard	● For stuffing, mix capers and mustard. Place about *1 tablespoon* stuffing mixture atop each of *4* patties. Spread to within ½ inch of edges. Top with remaining patties. Press meat around edges to seal well.
2 slices Swiss cheese 4 spinach leaves 4 kaiser rolls, split and toasted	● Place patties on an unheated rack in a broiler pan. Broil 3 to 4 inches from the heat about 13 minutes total till done, turning once. *Or,* grill patties, on an uncovered grill, directly over *medium-hot* coals for 13 to 14 minutes total, turning once. Top burgers with cheese. Heat just till cheese melts. Serve burgers on spinach-lined kaiser rolls. Serves 4.

Capers add a lively pickled flavor to just about anything, including these stuffed burgers. The tiny, olive green pods are flower buds picked before the petals can open and then soaked in vinegar or salt.

Blue Cheese Burgers

1 beaten egg 1 tablespoon Worcestershire sauce ⅓ cup fine dry rye bread crumbs 1 teaspoon prepared mustard ⅛ teaspoon pepper Dash garlic powder 1½ pounds lean ground beef	● In a medium mixing bowl combine egg and Worcestershire sauce. Stir in rye bread crumbs, mustard, pepper, and garlic powder. Add ground beef and mix well. Shape the meat mixture into twelve ¼-inch-thick patties.
¾ cup crumbled blue cheese	● Place about *2 tablespoons* blue cheese atop each of *6* patties. Spread to within ½ inch of edges. Top with remaining patties. Press meat around the edges of patties to seal well.
6 hamburger buns, split and toasted Alfalfa sprouts	● Place patties on a rack in an unheated broiler pan. Broil 3 to 4 inches from the heat about 13 minutes total or till done, turning once. *Or,* grill patties, on an uncovered grill, directly over *medium-hot* coals for 13 to 14 minutes total or till done, turning once. Serve burgers on buns with alfalfa sprouts. Serves 6.

Deciphering the labels on ground beef packages can be confusing. Often packages are labeled ground round, ground sirloin, or ground chuck (ground round being the most lean, followed by sirloin, and then chuck).

When choosing meat for burgers, consider how you're going to cook them. For broiled burgers, consider buying ground chuck (the fat drains away during broiling). For barbecued burgers, choose leaner meat, so fat doesn't drip onto hot coals and cause flare-ups.

1 As the bread dough rises, make the filling. Toss together the mozzarella cheese, salami, chopped tomato, and Parmesan cheese.

Cheese and Salami Calzones

2 to 2½ cups all-purpose flour
1 package active dry yeast
1 teaspoon dried sage, crushed
½ teaspoon salt
¾ cup warm water (115° to 120°)
2 tablespoons cooking oil

● In large mixer bowl combine *1 cup* flour, the yeast, sage, and salt. Add warm water and oil. Beat with an electric mixer on low speed for ½ minute. Beat on high speed for 3 minutes. Stir in as much of the remaining flour as you can. On a floured surface, knead in enough remaining flour to make a moderately stiff dough that is smooth and elastic (6 to 8 minutes total). Place in a greased bowl; turn once. Cover; let rise in a warm place till double (45 to 55 minutes).

1½ cups shredded mozzarella cheese (6 ounces)
⅓ pound salami, chopped
1 small tomato, peeled, seeded, and chopped
⅓ cup grated Parmesan cheese
1 egg
1 teaspoon water

● Meanwhile, make filling. In a bowl toss together the shredded mozzarella cheese, chopped salami, chopped tomato, and grated Parmesan cheese. Set the filling aside. Punch dough down; divide into 6 pieces. Cover; let dough rest 10 minutes.
Roll each piece into a 7-inch circle. Spoon about *½ cup* filling onto half of each. Combine egg and water; moisten edges of dough. Fold circle in half; use tines of a fork to seal. Place on greased baking sheet. Prick tops; brush with egg mixture. Bake in a 375° oven for 25 to 30 minutes or till golden. Remove from baking sheet; cool on wire rack. Makes 6.

To make child-size calzones, divide the dough into *12* pieces. Roll each into a *5-inch* circle and fill with about ¼ *cup* of the filling.

2 Punch down the risen dough and divide it into six pieces. Cover the pieces and let rest for 10 minutes.

3 With a rolling pin roll each piece of dough into a 7-inch circle.

4 Spoon about ½ cup of the cheese mixture onto half of each circle of dough. Moisten edges of the dough with a mixture of the egg and water.

5 Fold the circle in half over the filling. Use the tines of a fork to seal the edges together so none of the filling leaks out as the calzones bake.

Design-Your-Own Pizza

Thin Pizza Crusts	● Prepare and partially bake the Thin Pizza Crusts.
Zesty Tomato Sauce	● Spread the Zesty Tomato Sauce over the hot pizza crusts.
1 pound bulk Italian sausage *or* ground beef, cooked and drained; 2 cups diced Canadian-style bacon *or* fully cooked ham; *or* 6 ounces pepperoni slices **Chopped onion, shredded carrot, sliced mush-rooms, sliced pitted ripe olives, sliced pimiento-stuffed olives, chopped green pepper, *or* snipped parsley** **2 to 3 cups shredded mozzarella, cheddar, Swiss, *or* Monterey Jack cheese *or* grated Parmesan cheese**	● Sprinkle your choice of sausage, ground beef, Canadian-style bacon, ham, or pepperoni; and onion, carrot, mush-rooms, olives, green pepper, or parsley atop the tomato sauce. Then add your choice of mozzarella, cheddar, Swiss, Monterey Jack, or Parmesan cheese. Return pizzas to the 425° oven and bake for 10 to 15 minutes longer or till bubbly. Makes 2 (12-inch) or 3 (10-inch) thin-crust pizzas.

Design pizza around tradi-tional toppings such as ham, sausage, and pepper-oni and not-so-traditional toppings such as carrots and parsley. If you use onion, green pepper, or mushrooms, cook them first in a small amount of water for 3 to 5 minutes or till they are crisp-tender and drain.

Zesty Tomato Sauce

1 cup chopped onion **1 clove garlic, minced** **2 tablespoons cooking oil**	● In a large saucepan cook onion and garlic in cooking oil till onion is tender.
1 16-ounce can tomatoes, cut up **1 6-ounce can tomato paste** **2 tablespoons snipped parsley** **1 bay leaf** **2 teaspoons dried basil, crushed** **1 teaspoon dried oregano, crushed** **Dash bottled hot pepper sauce**	● Add *undrained* tomatoes, tomato paste, snipped parsley, bay leaf, dried basil, dried oregano, bottled hot pepper sauce, and ½ teaspoon *salt*. Bring to boiling; reduce heat. Boil gently, uncovered, for 25 to 30 minutes or till tomato sauce reaches desired con-sistency, stirring occasionally. Remove bay leaf from the sauce. Makes 2¼ cups.

Herbs and hot pepper sauce give this Zesty Tomato Sauce a flavor that's just right for pizza. Make it ahead and freeze or refrigerate until you're ready to make pizza.

Thin Pizza Crusts

2½ to 3 cups all-purpose
　　flour
　1 package active dry yeast
　1 teaspoon salt
　1 cup warm water (115°
　　to 120°)
　2 tablespoons cooking oil

● In a mixer bowl combine *1¼ cups* of the all-purpose flour, yeast, and salt. Stir in warm water and cooking oil.
　Beat at low speed with electric mixer for ½ minute, scraping bowl constantly. Beat 3 minutes at high speed.
　Stir in as much remaining flour as you can mix in with a spoon.

● Turn out onto a lightly floured surface. Knead in enough remaining flour to make a moderately stiff dough that is smooth and elastic (6 to 8 minutes total). Cover dough and let rest 10 minutes.

● For 12-inch pizzas, divide dough in half. On a lightly floured surface roll each half into a 13-inch circle.
　For 10-inch pizzas, divide dough into thirds; roll each into an 11-inch circle.
　Transfer to greased 12-inch or 10-inch pizza pans or baking sheets. Build up edges slightly. Bake in a 425° oven about 12 minutes or till lightly browned.

● Add desired toppings. Bake for 10 to 15 minutes or till bubbly. Makes 2 (12-inch) or 3 (10-inch) thin pizza crusts.

Vigorously beat the dough mixture with a wooden spoon for 2 minutes.

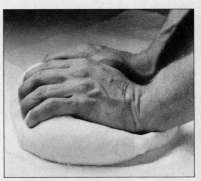

Knead on a floured surface till dough is smooth.

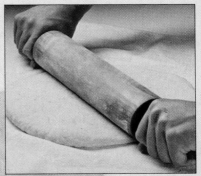

Divide dough into 2 or 3 portions. Roll into circles.

Put circles in pizza pans and crimp the edges by pinching dough between your fingers.

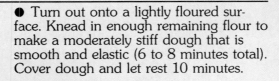

Creamy Lamb With Noodles

4 ounces medium noodles
1 pound boneless lamb
2 tablespoons butter *or* margarine

● Cook noodles according to package directions. Drain and keep warm. Meanwhile, bias-slice lamb into thin bite-size strips. In a skillet heat butter or margarine. Add lamb. Brown lamb, *half* at a time, on both sides. Return all lamb to the skillet.

1 4-ounce can mushroom stems and pieces, drained and chopped
½ cup sliced pitted ripe olives
1 tablespoon dried minced onion
¼ teaspoon dried oregano, crushed
⅛ teaspoon dried minced garlic
1 cup milk
2 teaspoons cornstarch

● Stir mushrooms, olives, onion, oregano, and garlic into lamb. Stir together milk and cornstarch. Stir into lamb mixture. Cook and stir till thickened and bubbly.

½ of an 8-ounce package cream cheese, cut up
¼ cup crumbled feta cheese
Snipped parsley (optional)

● Stir cream cheese and feta cheese into lamb mixture. Cook and stir about 2 minutes or till cheese is melted. Serve lamb mixture over noodles. Sprinkle with parsley, if desired. Serves 4.

To Italians, mozzarella cheese is matchless. To Wisconsin natives, cheddar is choice. But to Greeks, the sharp salty flavor of feta is first rate.

Pizza Fish Fillets

2	½-inch-thick bias-sliced pieces of French bread
	Butter *or* margarine
	Garlic powder
¼	cup shredded mozzarella cheese (1 ounce)

● Spread bread slices with butter or margarine. Sprinkle lightly with garlic powder. Place on the unheated rack of a broiler pan. Broil 4 inches from the heat for 1 to 2 minutes or till toasted. Sprinkle with cheese. Broil till cheese melts. Remove bread slices from broiler.

Savor the flavor of pizza, but this time with a new twist. Top toasted French bread with mozzarella cheese, tender fish, and pizza sauce.

2	individually frozen fish fillets (about 4 to 5 ounces each)
⅓	cup pizza sauce
¼	cup shredded mozzarella cheese (1 ounce)

● Place frozen fish fillets on rack of broiler pan. Broil fillets about 4 inches from the heat till fish flakes easily with a fork (allow 6 to 9 minutes for each ½ inch of thickness).
   Return toasted bread to broiler rack. Transfer 1 fillet to each slice of bread (see photo, below). Spoon sauce over fish. Sprinkle with cheese. Broil for 1 to 2 minutes more or till sauce is hot and cheese melts. Makes 2 servings.

To assemble, return the toasted French bread to the hot broiler rack. Use a spatula to transfer one fish fillet to each slice of bread.

Nutty Cheese Fondue

12 ounces process Swiss
cheese, shredded
(3 cups)
2 tablespoons all-purpose
flour
1 clove garlic, halved
1¼ cups dry white wine
1 tablespoon kirsch *or* dry
sherry (optional)
Dash ground red pepper

2 tablespoons chopped nuts
or sunflower nuts
1 loaf unsliced French, rye,
or whole wheat bread,
cubed

● In a medium bowl toss together
cheese and flour. Rub the inside of a
fondue pot with garlic. Discard garlic.
   In a medium saucepan heat wine over
medium heat till small bubbles rise to the
surface. Stir in cheese mixture little by
little, making sure cheese has melted
before adding more. (Stir constantly and
continue to add cheese till all is mixed
in.) Stir till cheese mixture bubbles gently.
Stir in kirsch, if desired, and red pepper.

● Pour cheese mixture into fondue pot.
Keep cheese mixture bubbling gently
over fondue burner. Sprinkle with nuts.
Serve with bread cubes. Serves 4 to 6.

Fondue comes from the
French word meaning "to
melt." And this pot of
creamy hot cheese is sure
to melt in your mouth.

If you have individual
slices of process Swiss
cheese, just tear the slices
into small pieces.

Four-Cheese Lasagna

6 ounces lasagna noodles	● In a large saucepan cook lasagna noodles according to package directions; drain. Set aside.
½ pound ground beef ½ cup chopped onion ⅓ cup chopped celery 1 clove garlic, minced	● In a large skillet cook ground beef, chopped onion, celery, and minced garlic till meat is brown and vegetables are tender. Drain off fat.
1½ teaspoons dried basil, crushed ¼ teaspoon dried oregano, crushed 1 3-ounce package cream cheese, cubed ⅓ cup light cream or milk	● Stir in the dried basil, dried oregano, ¼ teaspoon *salt*, and ⅛ teaspoon *pepper*. Add the cream cheese and light cream or milk. Cook and stir over low heat till cheese is melted.
½ cup dry white wine ½ cup shredded cheddar or gouda cheese (2 ounces)	● Stir in dry white wine. Gradually add the shredded cheddar or gouda cheese. Cook and stir till cheese is nearly melted; remove from heat.
1 cup cream-style cottage cheese 1 slightly beaten egg	● In small bowl stir together the cream-style cottage cheese and the slightly beaten egg.
6 ounces sliced mozzarella cheese	● Layer *half* of the cooked noodles in a greased 10x6x2-inch baking dish. Top with *half* of the meat sauce, *half* of the cottage cheese mixture, and *half* of the mozzarella cheese. Repeat layers. 　　Bake, uncovered, in a 375° oven for 30 to 35 minutes. Let stand 10 minutes before serving. Makes 6 servings.

This luscious main dish is a spin-off from an all-white lasagna that's popular in Spain. It boasts cheddar, cottage, mozzarella, and cream cheeses.

MICROWAVE TIMING
Micro-cook, uncovered, on HIGH for 10 to 12 minutes, turning dish once.

Crunchy New Orleans-Style Rice Patties

1½ cups cooked brown rice, slightly cooled
2 beaten eggs
½ cup sliced green onion
½ cup chopped walnuts
¼ cup fine dry bread crumbs
1 tablespoon chopped pimiento
½ teaspoon dried thyme, crushed
¼ teaspoon dried basil, crushed
⅛ teaspoon salt
  Several dashes ground red pepper

● In a medium bowl combine the cooked and slightly cooled brown rice, the beaten eggs, the sliced green onion, the chopped walnuts, the fine dry bread crumbs, the chopped pimiento, the dried thyme, the dried basil, the salt, and the ground red pepper.

Shape the rice mixture into eight ½-inch-thick patties. (Moisten hands to form patties, if necessary.)

2 tablespoons cooking oil

● In a large skillet over medium heat, fry the rice patties in hot cooking oil till golden brown, allowing 3 to 4 minutes per side. Remove to platter; keep warm.

¼ cup chopped green pepper
1 tablespoon butter *or* margarine
1 15½-ounce can red kidney beans
1 8-ounce can tomato sauce
1 teaspoon chili powder
1 cup shredded cheddar cheese (4 ounces)
¼ cup dairy sour cream

● Meanwhile, for sauce, in a saucepan cook green pepper in butter or margarine till tender. Stir in *undrained* beans, tomato sauce, and chili powder. Simmer, uncovered, about 6 minutes or till heated through. Mash beans slightly.

Spoon some of the bean mixture atop each patty. Sprinkle with some of the cheddar cheese and dollop with sour cream. Makes 4 servings.

Brown rice patties with red bean sauce was inspired by Creole red beans and rice. The New Orleans original was usually served on Mondays, which were washdays. The beans and rice cooked all day as folks waited for their laundry to dry. You don't have to wait all day to enjoy our version.

Spinach-Millet Soufflé

2 cups water **⅓ cup millet**	● Attach a foil collar to a 2-quart soufflé dish (*see hint, right*). Set aside. In saucepan combine water and millet. Simmer, covered, for 10 minutes; drain.
8 ounces fresh spinach *or* one 10-ounce package frozen chopped spinach	● In a saucepan, cook fresh spinach, covered, in a small amount of boiling salted water for 3 to 5 minutes. (*Or,* cook frozen spinach according to package directions.) Drain well.
¼ cup chopped onion **¼ cup butter *or* margarine** **¼ cup all-purpose flour** **¼ teaspoon ground nutmeg** **1 cup milk** **1½ cups shredded Swiss cheese (6 ounces)**	● In a saucepan cook onion in butter till the onion is tender but not brown. Stir in flour and nutmeg. Add milk all at once. Cook; stir till thickened and bubbly. Cook and stir 1 minute more. Remove from heat. Add cheese and cooked millet; stir to melt cheese. Stir in spinach.
6 egg yolks **6 egg whites**	● Beat egg yolks till thick and lemon-colored. Slowly add cheese mixture to egg yolks; stir constantly. Cool slightly. Using *clean* beaters, beat egg whites till stiff peaks form. Gradually pour yolk mixture over beaten whites, folding to blend. Turn out into prepared ungreased 2-quart soufflé dish.
	● Bake in a 350° oven for 50 to 55 minutes or till a knife inserted near center comes out clean. *Do not* open oven door till near the end of the baking time. Test soufflé while soufflé is in oven. Gently peel off collar; serve immediately. Serves 6.

To attach a foil collar to the soufflé dish, cut a piece of foil long enough to wrap around the dish with a 2- to 3-inch overlap. Fold foil into thirds lengthwise. Butter one side. Position foil around dish with buttered side in, letting collar extend 2 inches above top of dish; fasten with tape.

Cheesy Chicken Chowder

1 10-ounce package frozen mixed vegetables 1¾ cups chicken broth 1 medium onion, chopped (½ cup) 1 teaspoon prepared mustard ¼ teaspoon pepper	● In a large saucepan stir together frozen vegetables, chicken broth, onion, mustard, and pepper. Bring to boiling.
⅓ cup corkscrew macaroni *or* other small pasta	● Stir in macaroni. Reduce the heat. Simmer, covered, for 7 to 10 minutes or till pasta is tender, stirring occasionally.
1¾ cups milk 1 cup cubed cooked chicken 2 tablespoons all-purpose flour	● Stir in *1½ cups* of the milk and chicken. Stir remaining milk into flour till smooth. Stir into chicken mixture. Cook and stir till mixture is thickened and bubbly. Cook and stir for 1 minute more.
1 cup shredded process Swiss *or* sharp American cheese	● Add cheese. Cook and stir till cheese is melted. Makes 4 servings.

Few things warm the stomach or the soul as well as chicken noodle soup. Try our cheesy version. It's a creamy twist to a generation-jumping favorite.

Clam-Cheese Soup

1¼ cups milk
1 11-ounce can condensed cheddar cheese soup
1 7½-ounce can tomatoes, cut up
1 6½-ounce can minced clams
½ cup elbow *or* tiny shell macaroni
1 tablespoon dried diced green pepper
Bottled hot pepper sauce (optional)

● In a medium saucepan stir milk into soup. Stir in *undrained* tomatoes, *undrained* clams, macaroni, and green pepper. Bring to boiling. Reduce heat. Cover and simmer for 10 to 12 minutes or till macaroni is done. If desired, pass with hot pepper sauce. Makes 3 servings.

Keep these seven ingredients on hand and, presto, you'll have a delicious spur-of-the moment meal.

Nacho Potato Soup

2 cups water
1 10-ounce can tomatoes and green chili peppers
1 8-ounce can whole kernel corn
1 4¾-ounce package dry julienne potato mix
Several dashes bottled hot pepper sauce

● In a 3-quart saucepan combine water, *undrained* tomatoes, *undrained* corn, dry potatoes, seasoning mix from potato package, and hot pepper sauce. Bring mixture to boiling. Reduce heat. Cover and simmer about 15 minutes or till potatoes are tender, stirring occasionally.

Serve this hearty cheese, potato, and chicken soup with a crisp tossed salad for a quick dinner.

1½ cups diced cooked chicken
1 cup shredded American cheese (4 ounces)
½ cup sliced pitted olives
2 cups milk
Tortilla chips

● Stir in chicken, cheese, and olives. Cook and stir till cheese is melted. Stir in milk and cook till mixture is heated through, stirring occasionally. Serve with tortilla chips. Makes 6 servings

Mock Crab Chowder

½ of a 16-ounce package
loose-pack frozen
mixed broccoli, carrot,
cauliflower
¾ cup water
3 green onions, sliced
2 teaspoons instant chicken
bouillon granules

1½ cups milk *or* light cream
1 cup water
1 tablespoon cornstarch
1 3-ounce package cream
cheese, cubed
1 8-ounce package frozen
salad-style crab-
flavored fish

● Cut up any large vegetables. In a large saucepan combine vegetables, water, onions, and bouillon granules. Bring to boiling. Reduce heat. Cover and simmer over low heat for 5 to 7 minutes or till vegetables are crisp-tender.

● Stir in milk or cream. Stir water into cornstarch. Stir into vegetable mixture. Cook and stir till thickened and bubbly. Add cream cheese. Bring to boiling, stirring to melt cheese. Add crab-flavored fish. Heat through. Serves 3 or 4.

Frozen crab-flavored fish—a blend of pollock with some crabmeat or crab flavoring—is a tasty and inexpensive option to the real thing. When you buy it for Mock Crab Chowder, be sure to choose the salad-style type—it's a shredded-chunk form.

Speedy Taco Salad

1 pound ground beef *or*
   ground raw turkey
1 large onion, chopped
2 10-ounce cans tomatoes
   and green chili
   peppers
1 1¼-ounce package
   taco seasoning mix

● In a large skillet cook meat and onion till meat is brown and onion is tender. Drain off fat. Stir in tomatoes and green chili peppers and seasoning mix. Simmer, uncovered, for 8 to 10 minutes or to desired consistency.

For a really spicy meal, substitute Italian sausage for the beef or turkey.

½ head lettuce, shredded
2 cups shredded cheddar
   cheese (8 ounces)
2 medium tomatoes,
   chopped
8 pitted ripe olives, sliced
3 green onions, sliced
   Dairy sour cream
   Taco sauce
4 cups tortilla chips

● Set out lettuce, cheese, tomatoes, olives, onions, sour cream, and taco sauce. Arrange tortilla chips on 4 dinner plates. Spoon meat mixture over chips. Top meat mixture with desired toppings. Makes 4 servings.

Rice Salad Milano

1	**10-ounce package frozen white and wild rice**	● Place rice in pouch in a bowl of hot water. Let stand just till rice can be broken up. Remove rice from pouch, then use a fork to break up remaining pieces of rice.

Save the time it takes to cook rice for Rice Salad Milano by using frozen rice. It's precooked.

1	**6-ounce jar marinated artichoke hearts**
½	**of a small zucchini, halved lengthwise and thinly sliced**
1	**cup shredded cheddar cheese (4 ounces)**
4	**ounces sliced salami, cut into strips**
¼	**cup sliced pitted ripe olives**

● Meanwhile, drain artichokes, reserving marinade. Cut up any large artichokes.
In a large bowl toss together artichoke hearts, zucchini, cheddar cheese, salami strips, and olives.

Artichokes—relatives of the thistle—overcame a lackluster heritage to become gourmet fare.

2	**tablespoons white wine vinegar**
¾	**teaspoon dry mustard**
½	**teaspoon dried basil, crushed**
	Grated Parmesan cheese

● In a screw-top jar mix 2 tablespoons of the reserved marinade, vinegar, mustard, and basil. Cover. Shake well. Pour over vegetable mixture. Add rice. Toss well to coat. Cover and chill in the freezer for 10 minutes. Sprinkle each serving with cheese. Serves 3.

Prosciutto and Spinach Salad

½	**cup dairy sour cream**
1	**tablespoon milk**
⅛	**teaspoon garlic powder**
	Dash ground red pepper
¼	**cup finely shredded cucumber**
2	**tablespoons snipped chives _or_ sliced green onion**

● For dressing, in a small mixing bowl combine sour cream, milk, garlic powder, and pepper. Stir in cucumber and chives or green onion. Cover and chill in the freezer for 10 minutes.

Because Italian ham called prosciutto is highly seasoned, we call for it thinly sliced.

4	**cups torn spinach**
1	**15-ounce can garbanzo beans, drained**
1	**cup sliced fresh mushrooms**
1	**cup cubed cheddar cheese (4 ounces)**
2	**ounces very thinly sliced prosciutto _or_ smoked ham, cut into 1-inch strips**
8	**cherry tomatoes, halved**
	Herb-seasoned croutons

● In a large bowl combine spinach, garbanzo beans, mushrooms, cheddar cheese, prosciutto or smoked ham, and cherry tomatoes.
To serve, sprinkle salad with croutons. Toss salad with dressing. Serves 4.

Turkey 'n' Fruit Plate

**Assorted fresh fruit
(banana and kiwi fruit
slices, melon balls,
or pineapple and plum
wedges)
Lemon juice
Lettuce leaves**

● Wash fruit, if necessary. If using banana slices, dip them in lemon juice to prevent browning. Arrange fruit on 3 lettuce-lined plates.

**3 slices cheddar, Colby, *or*
Swiss cheese
1 6-ounce package (6 round
slices) sliced turkey
luncheon meat
½ cup lemon *or* orange
yogurt
2 tablespoons mayonnaise
or salad dressing
1 tablespoon milk
½ teaspoon poppy seed
Breadsticks (optional)**

● Cut cheese into strips. Divide cheese strips among turkey slices. Roll turkey slices around cheese strips. Arrange on plates next to fruit.

In a small bowl stir together lemon or orange yogurt, mayonnaise or salad dressing, milk, and poppy seed. Drizzle over fruit and turkey rolls. Serve with breadsticks, if desired. Makes 3 servings.

**This recipe makes a
refreshing hot weather
meal. If your favorite fruit
isn't in season, use frozen
or drained canned fruit.**

Three-Bean Pasta Salad

1½ cups corkscrew *or* small shell macaroni

● Cook macaroni according to package directions. Drain. Transfer to a bowl of *ice water.* Let stand for 5 minutes. Drain thoroughly.

1 pint three-bean salad, *or* one 15- *or* 17-ounce can three-bean salad
1 cup cubed *or* shredded cheddar cheese (4 ounces)
6 ounces thinly sliced boiled ham, cut into bite-size strips
1 medium carrot, thinly bias sliced
4 lettuce cups

● Meanwhile, in a large bowl combine three-bean salad, cheese, ham, and carrot. Add macaroni. Toss well to coat. Chill in the freezer for 15 minutes. Serve in lettuce cups. Makes 4 servings.

Toss in macaroni, cheese, and ham, and a salad becomes a great one-dish meal. Now, that's using your bean!

Beef and Greens Toss

5 cups torn spinach
1 pint creamy coleslaw
8 ounces thinly sliced cooked beef, cut into bite-size strips
2 slices Swiss cheese, cut into thin strips
1 cup cherry tomatoes, halved

● In a large salad bowl toss together spinach, coleslaw, beef, Swiss cheese, and tomatoes. Toss mixture well to coat. Makes 4 servings.

Maryellyn, one of our Test Kitchen home economists, says, "This salad is a favorite in the Test Kitchen because the coleslaw adds a nice crunch. And there is no need for extra salad dressing!"

Stuffed French Toast

1 **8-ounce package cream cheese, softened** 1 **teaspoon vanilla** ½ **cup chopped walnuts**	● In a small mixer bowl beat the cream cheese and vanilla on medium speed of an electric mixer till fluffy. Stir in chopped walnuts.
1 **16-ounce loaf French bread**	● Cut the French bread into ten to twelve 1½-inch-thick slices. Cut a pocket in the top of each slice (see tip, opposite). Fill *each* pocket with about *1½ tablespoons* of the cheese mixture.
4 **beaten eggs** 1 **cup whipping cream** ½ **teaspoon vanilla** ½ **teaspoon ground nutmeg**	● In a small bowl stir together the eggs, whipping cream, vanilla, and nutmeg. Dip bread slices in egg mixture, being careful not to squeeze out filling. Cook in a lightly greased electric skillet or griddle till golden brown, turning once. Keep cooked slices hot in a 200° oven while cooking the remainder.
1 **12-ounce jar apricot preserves** ½ **cup orange juice**	● Meanwhile, in a small saucepan heat together the apricot preserves and orange juice, stirring frequently. To serve, drizzle apricot sauce over the hot French toast. Makes 10 to 12 stuffed slices.

Surprise your family by making something familiar, yet different, for breakfast or brunch this weekend—Stuffed French Toast. It's familiar because the bread is dipped and fried just like ordinary French toast. And it's different because it's stuffed with a delicious cream cheese and nut filling.

1 Cut a pocket in the top of each bread slice by using the point of a sharp knife to cut from the top almost to the bottom of the slice. Cut across the top of the slice, but do not cut the sides of the slice. Fill each pocket with cream cheese mixture.

2 Dip the filled bread slices in the egg mixture, being careful not to squeeze out the cream cheese mixture. Be sure to dip both sides of the bread slice.

3 Cook the filled bread slices in a lightly greased electric skillet or griddle till both sides are golden brown, turning once.

1 Cut the shortening into the flour mixture till the mixture resembles coarse crumbs. The best utensils to use for cutting in shortening are a pastry blender or two knives. Mixing by hand tends to soften the shortening, making a sticky, difficult-to-handle dough.

2 Gently push the flour-shortening mixture against the edges of the bowl, making a well. Add the milk all at once, pouring it into the well.

3 Using a fork, stir the mixture quickly. Stir just till the mixture follows the fork around the bowl and forms a soft dough.

4 Turn the dough out onto a lightly floured surface. Knead gently for 10 to 12 strokes (see tip at right). This helps to develop the biscuit's structure and distributes the moisture to make the biscuits more flaky.

5 On the lightly floured surface pat the dough to ½-inch thickness (or use a lightly floured rolling pin). Sprinkle the dough with a little flour, if necessary, to keep the dough from sticking.

6 Cut the dough with a 2½-inch biscuit cutter or a 2½-inch-wide glass. Dip the cutter in flour between cuts to prevent sticking. Press the cutter straight down to get evenly shaped biscuits. Transfer the biscuits to an ungreased baking sheet.

Cheese-Herb Biscuits

2 cups all-purpose flour
1 tablespoon baking powder
2 teaspoons sugar
½ teaspoon dried oregano, basil, savory, *or* marjoram, crushed
½ teaspoon cream of tartar
¼ teaspoon salt

● In a large bowl stir together the 2 cups flour; baking powder; sugar; dried oregano, dried basil, dried savory, or dried marjoram; cream of tartar; and salt.

½ cup shortening
½ cup shredded cheddar, Swiss, *or* Monterey Jack cheese (2 ounces)

● Use a pastry blender or two knives to cut the shortening into the flour mixture till the mixture resembles coarse crumbs. Stir in cheese. Gently push the mixture against the edges of the bowl, making a well in the center.

⅔ cup milk
All-purpose flour

● Pour the milk into the well. Use a fork to stir just till dough clings together. Knead on a lightly floured surface for 10 to 12 strokes. Pat to ½-inch thickness. Cut with a 2½-inch biscuit cutter, dipping cutter in flour between cuts. Pat scraps together, cut with biscuit cutter. Transfer cut biscuits to an ungreased baking sheet. Bake in a 450° oven for 10 to 12 minutes or till golden. Serve warm. Makes 8 to 10 biscuits.

If these Cheese-Herb Biscuits don't turn out first-rate, it's probably because you undermixed or overmixed the dough. Not mixing or kneading the dough enough will give you biscuits that are small and rough with a spotted crust. The inside will be coarse instead of flaky. If you mix or knead the dough too much, the biscuits will be tough, dry, and have a peak on top.

The best way to avoid these problems is to follow the recipe closely. Be sure to stir the dough just till it clings together. And knead it only 10 to 12 strokes. When you're done, the biscuit dough should be well mixed but not elastic.

Kneading Biscuits

Properly kneading dough mixes the ingredients and helps give structure to biscuits and other breads. Kneading is a technique that you can master with a little practice. Turn the dough out onto a lightly floured surface. Curve your fingers over the dough and use the heel of your hand to pull the dough toward you and then push it away. Rotate the dough a quarter-turn, fold it over, and repeat the process.

Wheat and Cheese Spirals

2 cups whole wheat flour 2 teaspoons baking powder ¼ teaspoon salt	● In a mixing bowl stir together the whole wheat flour, the baking powder, and the salt.
½ cup butter *or* margarine	● Cut in ½ cup butter or margarine till mixture resembles coarse crumbs.
1 beaten egg ⅔ cup milk	● Make a well in the center. Combine egg and milk; add all at once to dry ingredients. Stir just till dough clings together. Knead gently on a lightly floured surface for 12 to 15 strokes. Roll dough into a 15x6-inch rectangle.
½ cup shredded Monterey Jack cheese with jalapeño peppers Melted butter *or* margarine Sesame seed, poppy seed, toasted wheat germ, *or* dillseed	● Sprinkle cheese over dough. Fold dough in half lengthwise to make a 15x3-inch rectangle. Cut into fifteen 3x1-inch strips. Holding a strip at both ends, twist in opposite directions twice to form a spiral. Place on lightly greased baking sheet, pressing both ends down. Brush with melted butter; sprinkle with sesame seed, poppy seed, toasted wheat germ, or dillseed. Bake in a 450° oven for 8 to 10 minutes. Serve warm. Makes 15 spirals.

Monterey Jack cheese with jalapeño peppers adds a little zing to Wheat and Cheese Spirals. You may be fooled when you bite into them. They have the tender texture of yeast breads, but are actually made like biscuits. Serve them with soups or salads. On their own, they're great as snacks.

Swiss Rye Bread

1½ to 1¾ cups all-purpose flour 1 package active dry yeast	● In a large mixer bowl combine *1 cup* of the flour and the yeast.
1 cup milk 1 tablespoon sugar ¾ teaspoon salt ¾ cup shredded Swiss *or* cheddar cheese (3 ounces)	● In saucepan heat milk, sugar, and salt just till warm (115° to 120°); stir constantly. Add to flour mixture; add cheese. Beat at low speed of electric mixer ½ minute, scraping sides of bowl constantly. Beat 3 minutes at high speed.
¾ cup rye flour *or* triticale flour	● Using a spoon, stir in rye or triticale flour and as much of the remaining all-purpose flour as you can. Turn out onto lightly floured surface. Knead in enough of the remaining all-purpose flour to make a moderately stiff dough that is smooth and elastic (6 to 8 minutes total). Shape into a ball. Place in a lightly greased bowl; turn once to grease surface. Cover; let rise in a warm place till double (55 to 60 minutes).
	● Punch down. Cover; let rest 10 minutes. Shape into a loaf. Place in a greased 8x4x2-inch loaf pan. Cover; let rise till nearly double (35 to 40 minutes).
	● Bake in a 375° oven for 30 to 35 minutes. If necessary, cover top of loaf with foil during last 15 minutes of baking to prevent overbrowning. Remove from pan; cool on wire rack. Makes 1 loaf.

Start the day with a slice of toasted Swiss Rye Bread—for a change from cold cereal. Choose Swiss or cheddar cheese to team up with the distinctive flavor provided by rye or triticale flour.

Blueberry Bites

½ cup butter *or* margarine, softened
1 3-ounce package cream cheese, softened
1 cup all-purpose flour

● For tart shells, in a small mixer bowl beat together butter or margarine and cream cheese. Add flour and beat well. Cover and chill dough about 1 hour.

In a hurry? Skip making the blueberry filling. With the variety of canned pie fillings available, there are lots of other tarts you can prepare. Cherry, raisin, strawberry, and red raspberry are just a few of the possibilities.

2 tablespoons brown sugar
1 tablespoon cornstarch
2 cups fresh *or* frozen blueberries, thawed
2 teaspoons lemon juice

● Meanwhile, for blueberry filling, in a medium saucepan combine brown sugar and cornstarch. Mash blueberries slightly, then add blueberries and lemon juice to saucepan. Cook and stir till thickened and bubbly, then cook and stir for 2 minutes more. Remove from heat. Cover with waxed paper. Cool.

Whipped cream (optional)

● Divide dough into 24 balls. Place each ball in an ungreased 1¾-inch muffin cup. Press dough evenly against bottom and sides of cup. (See photo, below.) Fill *each* pastry-lined muffin cup with about *2 teaspoons* of blueberry filling. Bake in a 325° oven for 20 to 25 minutes or till lightly browned. Cool slightly. Remove from pan. Cool completely on a wire rack. Just before serving, dollop with whipped cream, if desired. Makes 24.

Be sure to press the dough *evenly* against bottoms and sides of the muffin cups. If the dough is too thin at any one place, the tarts may crack as they bake and allow the filling to leak through.

Brandy Tarts

½ cup butter *or* margarine, softened
1 3-ounce package cream cheese, softened
1 cup all-purpose flour

● For tart shells, in a small mixer bowl beat together butter or margarine and cream cheese. Add flour and beat well. Cover and chill dough about 1 hour.

Here's a great make-ahead idea: Wrap and freeze the petite cream cheese tart shells after they're baked and cooled. Then pull them out of the freezer just before you're ready to make the filling.

● Divide dough into 24 balls. Place each ball in an ungreased 1¾-inch muffin cup. Press dough evenly against bottom and sides of cup. (See photo, left.) Bake in a 325° oven for 20 to 25 minutes or till lightly browned. Cool slightly. Remove from pan. Cool completely on a wire rack.

1 package 4-serving-size *instant* chocolate *or* vanilla pudding mix
2 tablespoons brandy
1 tablespoon crème de cacao
½ of a 4-ounce container frozen whipped dessert topping, thawed

● Meanwhile, for filling, prepare pudding mix according to package directions, *except* use 1 cup milk. Stir in brandy and crème de cacao. Fold dessert topping into pudding mixture.

¼ cup chopped pistachios *or* pecans

● Spoon filling into cooled tart shells. Sprinkle with nuts. Chill thoroughly. Makes 24.

Whole Wheat-Fruit Shortcake

1 cup all-purpose flour
¾ cup whole wheat *or* triticale flour
¼ cup sugar
1 tablespoon baking powder
¼ teaspoon salt
¼ teaspoon ground nutmeg
⅛ teaspoon ground ginger
½ cup butter *or* margarine
1 beaten egg
⅔ cup milk
¾ cup cooked wheat berries

● In a mixing bowl stir together all-purpose flour, whole wheat or triticale flour, sugar, baking powder, salt, nutmeg, and ginger. Cut in butter or margarine till mixture resembles coarse crumbs.

Combine beaten egg and milk. Add all at once to flour mixture. Add wheat berries, stirring just till moistened. Spread dough in two greased 8x1½-inch round baking pans.

Bake in a 450° oven for 10 to 12 minutes or till done. Cool shortcake in pans for 10 minutes. Remove from pans; cool on wire rack.

3 cups fresh fruit
Lemon juice (optional)
Cream Filling (see recipe, right)
Honey (optional)

● Slice or halve fruit as desired. If using bananas, pears, peaches, or apples, dip slices in lemon juice to prevent browning.

Place one of the shortcake layers on a serving plate, flat side up. Spread *half* of the Cream Filling atop layer. Arrange *half* of the sliced fruit atop filling. Place the top layer of shortcake on the fruit, rounded side up. Top with the remaining filling and fruit. Drizzle honey atop shortcake, if desired. Cut into wedges to serve. Makes 8 servings.

Cream Filling:
In a small mixer bowl beat one 3-ounce package softened *cream cheese* till smooth and fluffy. Add one 8-ounce carton *vanilla yogurt;* beat at low speed till well combined. Cover and chill. Makes 1¼ cups.

Choose-a-Flavor Cheesecake

¾ **cup all-purpose flour**
3 **tablespoons brown sugar**
  or **sugar**
⅓ **cup butter**
1 **slightly beaten egg yolk**
1 **teaspoon vanilla**

● Preheat oven to 375°. In a bowl combine flour and the 3 tablespoons sugar; cut in butter till crumbly. Add egg yolk and 1 teaspoon vanilla; mix well. Pat ⅓ of dough on bottom of an 8-inch springform pan (or a 9-inch pie plate).

● Pat remaining dough onto sides of springform pan to a height of 1¼ inches (*or,* pat remaining dough up sides of pie plate); set aside.

1 **8-ounce package cream**
  cheese, softened
½ **cup packed brown sugar**
  or **sugar**
1 **teaspoon vanilla**
2 **eggs**
1½ **cups dairy sour cream**

● In a small mixer bowl beat softened cream cheese till fluffy. Add the ½ cup sugar and 1 teaspoon vanilla; beat well. Add eggs; beat at low speed with electric mixer just till combined. (Do not overbeat.) Stir in sour cream.

The brown sugar in this recipe gives the cheesecake a praline-like flavor. To test the doneness of cheesecake, insert a knife near the center of the cake. If it comes out clean, the cake is done.

Strawberry *or* **Raspberry Glaze, Orange Topper, Blueberry Topper,** *or* 1 **cup dairy sour cream**

● Turn into crust-lined springform pan. Bake in the 375° oven 35 to 40 minutes for springform pan (35 minutes for pie plate) or till center appears set. Cool 15 minutes on wire rack. Loosen sides of cheesecake from springform pan with a spatula. Cool 30 minutes; remove sides of pan. Cool completely. (If you use a pie plate, cool cheesecake completely in pie plate.) Chill thoroughly. Spread desired topper or glaze atop cheesecake. Makes 8 to 10 servings.

● **Orange Topper:** Drain and reserve liquid from one 11-ounce can *mandarin orange sections;* add enough *orange juice* to liquid to make ½ cup liquid; set aside liquid and orange sections. In saucepan combine ¼ cup *sugar* and 2 teaspoons *cornstarch.* Stir in the ½ cup liquid. Cook and stir over medium heat till thickened and bubbly. Cook and stir 2 minutes more. Gradually stir hot mixture into 1 beaten *egg yolk;* return to saucepan. Cook and stir till bubbly. Remove from heat. Stir in 1 tablespoon *butter* and ¼ teaspoon *vanilla.* Cover surface with clear plastic wrap. Cool. Spoon sauce atop cheesecake and arrange orange sections atop sauce.

Cheesecake is traditionally made in a springform pan like this one, but you can also make this recipe in a 9-inch pie plate.

Blueberry Topper: Stir 1 to 2 tablespoons brandy or your favorite liqueur into *half* of a 21-ounce can blueberry pie filling.

We designed this cheesecake to suit your fancy. Take your pick from Orange Topper, plain sour cream dusted with ground cinnamon, Strawberry or Raspberry Glaze, and Blueberry Topper.

Strawberry or Raspberry Glaze:
Thaw and drain one 10-ounce package *frozen sliced strawberries* or *red raspberries*; reserve syrup. In a saucepan combine ¼ cup *sugar* and 1 tablespoon *cornstarch*. Add water to syrup to make ⅔ cup liquid; add to saucepan. Cook and stir till mixture is thickened and bubbly; cook and stir 2 minutes more. Remove from heat; stir in drained strawberries or raspberries and 1 tablespoon *lemon juice*. Cover surface with clear plastic wrap. Cool.

Index